DK SUPER Planet

Essential
ECOSYSTEMS

Journey around the world to discover the rich and diverse ecosystems that make up our beautiful planet—from tropical rainforests, to sun-drenched savannas, to vibrant coral reefs

Produced for DK by
Editorial Just Content Limited
Design Studio Noel

Author Lola M. Schaefer

Senior Editor Amelia Jones
Senior Art Editor Gilda Pacitti
Managing Editor Katherine Neep
Managing Art Editor Sarah Corcoran
Production Editor Jaypal Chauhan
Production Controller Rebecca Parton
Publisher Sarah Forbes
Managing Director, Learning Hilary Fine

First American Edition, 2025
Published in the United States by DK Publishing,
a division of Penguin Random House LLC
1745 Broadway, 20th Floor, New York, NY 10019

Copyright © 2025 Dorling Kindersley Limited
25 26 27 28 29 10 9 8 7 6 5 4 3 2 1
001–345411–Mar/2025

All rights reserved.
Without limiting the rights under the copyright reserved above, no part of this publication may be reproduced, stored in or introduced into a retrieval system, or transmitted, in any form, or by any means (electronic, mechanical, photocopying, recording, or otherwise), without the prior written permission of the copyright owner.
Published in Great Britain by Dorling Kindersley Limited

A catalog record for this book
is available from the Library of Congress.
HC ISBN: 978-0-5939-6260-2
PB ISBN: 978-0-5939-6259-6

DK books are available at special discounts when purchased in bulk for sales promotions, premiums, fund-raising, or educational use.
For details, contact: DK Publishing Special Markets,
1745 Broadway, 20th Floor, New York, NY 10019
SpecialSales@dk.com

Printed and bound in China

www.dk.com

Contents

What is an Ecosystem?	4
Vital Ecosystems	6
Tropical Rainforests and Cloud Forests	8
Case Study: The Amazon	10
Temperate Forests	12
Case Study: The Taiga	14
Grasslands and Savannas	16
Case Study: The Serengeti	18
Freshwater Ecosystems	20
Case Study: The Ganges	22
Marine Ecosystems	24
Case Study: The Great Barrier Reef	26
Desert Ecosystems	28
Case Study: The Sahara	30
Helping Ecosystems	32
Everyday Science: Taking the Wolves out of Yellowstone	34
Everyday Science: Rewilding Yellowstone	36
Let's Experiment! Building for Bees	38
Let's Experiment! Make a Bird Feeder	40
Vocabulary Builder: What Does an Ecologist Do?	42
Glossary	44
Index	46

Words in **bold** are explained in the glossary on page 44.

What is an ECOSYSTEM?

Plants and animals live in a variety of **habitats**. These habitats make up different **ecosystems**. An ecosystem is a community of living (**biotic**) things, such as plants and animals. They interact with non-living (**abiotic**) things, like rocks, in their environment. These include sunlight, water, air, and soil. A healthy ecosystem provides everything that the plants and animals need to survive.

Foxes live in a wide variety of habitats and can be found on every **continent** of the world, except for Antarctica. They live in rural areas such as **forests**, **grasslands**, and deserts, but they are common in towns and cities, too.

A cave is an ecosystem. Mosses and algae grow in the cool, humid environment. Spiders and centipedes have plenty of rocks to hide under. The plants and animals who live there thrive in the darkness.

In a balanced ecosystem, plants and animals can meet all their needs.

Fascinating fact

Puddles are full of microorganisms, such as bacteria, protozoa, and algae.

A rotting log is an ecosystem. When a tree dies, it starts to decay. This can provide a home for other living things, like mushrooms and insects.

When toucans eat fruits and berries, the seeds are spread widely across the land. This helps new plants grow.

Male pufferfish build special nests on the ocean floor. Female pufferfish place their eggs in the center of the nest. This ecosystem allows the pufferfish to reproduce.

Vital ECOSYSTEMS

Essential to all life on Earth, ecosystems are home to a huge variety of plant and animal **species**. They clean our air and water. And they provide rich soil for growing crops. Different ecosystems provide us with rock and wood for construction. They also provide plants and oils for fuel.

Tundras regulate Earth's climate. They reflect sunlight away from Earth. They trap heat in the sea so it does not warm the air.

Find out!

More than 60 years ago, **ecologist** Rachel Carson wrote a book about dangers to ecosystems. Can you find out the name of the book?

Silent Spring.

Forests provide us with wood. This resource can be used for fuel and building. Trees we cut down grow back slowly over time.

Ecosystems provide us with opportunities for different kinds of recreation. These include zip-lining, swimming, exploring caves, rockclimbing, boating, and many more!

Some ecosystems can reduce damage from natural disasters. For example, flood plains prevent **rivers** from rising and destroying property.

Scientists study ecosystems. For example, **oceanographers** study what harms living things in ocean ecosystems and how to keep oceans healthy.

Tropical rainforests are ecosystems with incredible **biodiversity.** They have everything the plants and animals that live there need to survive.

7

Tropical Rainforests and CLOUD FORESTS

Rainforests and **cloud forests** are both tropical forests. But they have some major differences. Tropical rainforests are hot, humid, and rainy. Cloud forests are cooler. Their **canopy**, or tree cover, is not as thick. And they tend to be found in mountainous areas. The trees in a forest ecosystem produce oxygen. Both rainforests and cloud forests are high in biodiversity.

The cloud forests of Central America are home to many unique species.

The resplendent quetzal has green **iridescent** feathers. It can easily **camouflage** itself among the bright leaves of the cloud forest's canopy.

Cloud forests are home to different species of spikethumb frogs. They live near **streams**. The Honduras spikethumb frog is critically **endangered**.

Some amazing animals live in the Sumatran tropical rainforest.

Fascinating fact

During one day of **photosynthesis**, a mature oak tree releases over 72 gallons (274 liters) of oxygen into the air. This is half of the oxygen you need in one day.

Sumatran orangutans live in the trees. They very rarely travel on the ground. They are critically endangered.

The Sumatran tiger is also a critically endangered animal. It is the last surviving species of island tiger in the world.

The Sumatran clouded leopard has large paws and special footpads. These allow it to climb up and down trees easily.

Case Study: THE AMAZON

The world's largest rainforest is the Amazon. Located mainly in Brazil in South America, it is also the most **diverse** ecosystem on Earth. More than 3 million species live there. Thanks to the amount of rain, the hot temperatures, and the number of rivers and streams, plants and animals in the Amazon have everything they need to survive.

In the past, people cut down almost 20 percent of the rainforest. But today, there are **conservation** efforts to stop **deforestation** in the Amazon.

Capybaras are very social, living in large groups and mixing with other animals. They love to swim and communicate with each other using barks, whistles, and purrs.

The Amazon giant water lily can grow up to 10 ft (3 m) across. Its long stalk anchors it to the river bottom. Its huge leaves absorb sunlight.

Leaf-cutter ants can cut and carry 10 times their weight in leaves. They store leaves so they will rot. The rotten leaves fertilize fungus that the ant larvae eat.

The cacao tree produces pods. Each pod has 30–50 cocoa beans inside it. This makes enough chocolate for one 3-ounce (85 g) bar.

Find out!

Can you find out how many insect species there are in the Amazon rainforest?

Scientists estimate over 2.5 million.

Arapaima are one of the largest freshwater fish in the world. They can grow up to 10 ft (3 m) long and weigh as much as 440 pounds (200 kg).

Temperate FORESTS

Temperate forests are **woodland** ecosystems. They experience all four seasons. They might have evergreen conifers or deciduous trees, or both. Deciduous trees lose their leaves in winter. Evergreen trees keep their leaves year-round. A wide variety of plants and animals live in this ecosystem. Temperate rainforests are one type of temperate forest. They exist in only a few places on Earth.

Mountain beavers are rodents. They need to drink up to one-third of their weight in water every day.

Fascinating fact

Snowshoe hares live in temperate forests. Their fur changes color to help them camouflage, changing from brown in the warmer months to white in the winter.

Coast redwoods are huge trees. They can live for more than 2,000 years and grow over 300 ft (91 m) tall.

TEMPERATE RAINFORESTS

- Near coasts
- Moderate temperatures
- Rain, snow, sleet, and fog
- Four **seasons**
- Trees with needles, some trees with leaves
- Shrubs, berries, mosses, and ferns

Both temperate and tropical rainforests have high **humidity**, unique plants and animals, biodiversity, and heavy rainfall.

TROPICAL RAINFORESTS

- Near the **equator**
- Hot temperatures
- Rain and fog
- Two seasons, wet and dry
- Trees with wide, waxy leaves
- Soft-stemmed plants, short trees, and shrubs

13

Case Study:
THE TAIGA

Earth's largest ecosystem is the taiga, or boreal forest, which is located in the **Arctic** zone. It covers the northern parts of three continents—North America, Europe, and Asia. The taiga has an extremely cold climate. Most of the year, it is covered in snow. A layer of permanently frozen soil covers its surface. Animals and plants have developed **adaptations** to survive there.

Being so far north, the sky over the taiga is often lit up by the **northern lights**.

The Canadian lynx has adapted to the snow and ice. It has large snowshoe-shaped paws, thick fur, and fur-covered feet.

Fascinating fact

The taiga covers 6.6 million square miles (17 million sq km). It is almost 12 percent of Earth's land area.

A muskeg is a bog found in the North American taiga. This ecosystem supports woodland beavers, muskrats, and caribou.

The conifers in the taiga form a thick canopy. Lichens, mushrooms, and mosses cover the shady forest floor.

Brown bears thrive in the taiga ecosystem. They eat a variety of animals and plants, and have thick fur to keep them warm during the very cold winters.

Fireweed is a plant that has adapted to life in the taiga. It grows quickly during the short summer and disperses its seeds.

The purple pitcher plant has adapted to grow in the taiga's bogs. As insects land on it, they slide down into its deep leaves. The plant then digests them.

Grasslands and
SAVANNAS

There are two main types of grasslands: temperate grasslands and tropical **savannas**. These ecosystems are known for their wide, open expanses of grasses and shrubs. They have few trees and get little rainfall. Temperate grasslands have four seasons. Savannas only have two. Grasslands support a variety of plants and animals. The Great Plains in the US is a temperate grassland.

Prairie dogs are famous residents of the Great Plains. They use their voices to communicate and can alert each other to threats.

The plains bison lives on the vegetation of the Great Plains. There are only around 45,000 of these animals left today.

Fascinating fact

Lots of grasses in grasslands have very deep root systems. If there is a fire, grass can regrow quickly from the undamaged roots.

The Australian savanna is home to a variety of plants and animals.

The brushtail possum is a small marsupial. It thrives in many environments, including the savanna. It mostly eats leaves, but sometimes eats small mammals.

The eucalyptus tree's thick bark protects it from dry summers and fire. Each year, the tree grows a new layer of bark and sheds the oldest layer.

Whiptail wallabies are social animals. They form groups of up to 50. The wallabies take turns looking out for **predators** while others rest.

Case Study: THE SERENGETI

In Tanzania, a vast plain of open savanna is known as the Serengeti. Its fertile land is home to many animals. These include herds of **prey** animals and the predators who eat them. But the Serengeti faces threats, including illegal hunting and wildfires. Today, there are efforts to conserve this amazing ecosystem and protect the animals that live there.

Visiting and spending money in threatened natural areas like the Serengeti can help conserve them. This is called ecotourism.

Find out!

Find out the names of three endangered mammals that live in the Serengeti. Why do their populations keep decreasing?

The black rhinoceros, African elephant, and African wild dog are all decreasing. They are losing their habitats and being hunted.

18

Every year, more than 1.5 million wildebeest migrate 500 miles (800 km). They start in the Serengeti and travel north. Then, they return south.

Carnivores, like lions, hunt the many **herbivores** who live in the Serengeti. These predator–prey relationships keep the ecosystem balanced.

Oxpeckers and rhinoceroses have a special relationship. These small birds eat parasites, ticks, and insects off a rhinoceros's body. They also make noise if an enemy is near, which alerts the rhinoceros to danger.

In the Serengeti, poachers try to hunt "the Big Five." The Big Five refers to leopards, lions, rhinoceroses, elephants, and African buffaloes. Rangers patrol the park. They arrest any poachers they find.

Freshwater
ECOSYSTEMS

All living things need water to survive. Many plants and animals need to live in or near fresh water in freshwater ecosystems. These include rivers, streams, **lakes**, and **wetlands**. Freshwater ecosystems are rare. They cover less than 0.01 percent of Earth's surface.

Sunlight warms water in freshwater ecosystems and causes it to **evaporate**. The water rises as water vapor and forms clouds. Water droplets in the clouds cool and **condense** until rain or snow falls to Earth. This cycle replenishes fresh water on Earth.

Scientists who study freshwater ecosystems are called limnologists. They test the water for pollutants. They decide how to keep these habitats healthy.

A **pond** is a freshwater ecosystem. It supports plants and animals in a **food chain**.

Fascinating fact

Although small, ponds often have more biodiversity than rivers and lakes.

1 Water lilies use sunlight, water, air, and minerals to thrive. They are the **producers** in this food chain.

2 **Primary consumers**, such as snails, tadpoles, insects, and small fish, eat the producers.

3 **Secondary consumers**, like amphibians, reptiles, and some fish, eat primary consumers.

4 **Tertiary consumers**, such as birds, people, and other mammals, eat primary and secondary consumers. They are at the top of the food chain.

5 **Decomposers**, like bacteria, fungi, and scavengers, break down dead plants and animals. They recycle the nutrients into the soil.

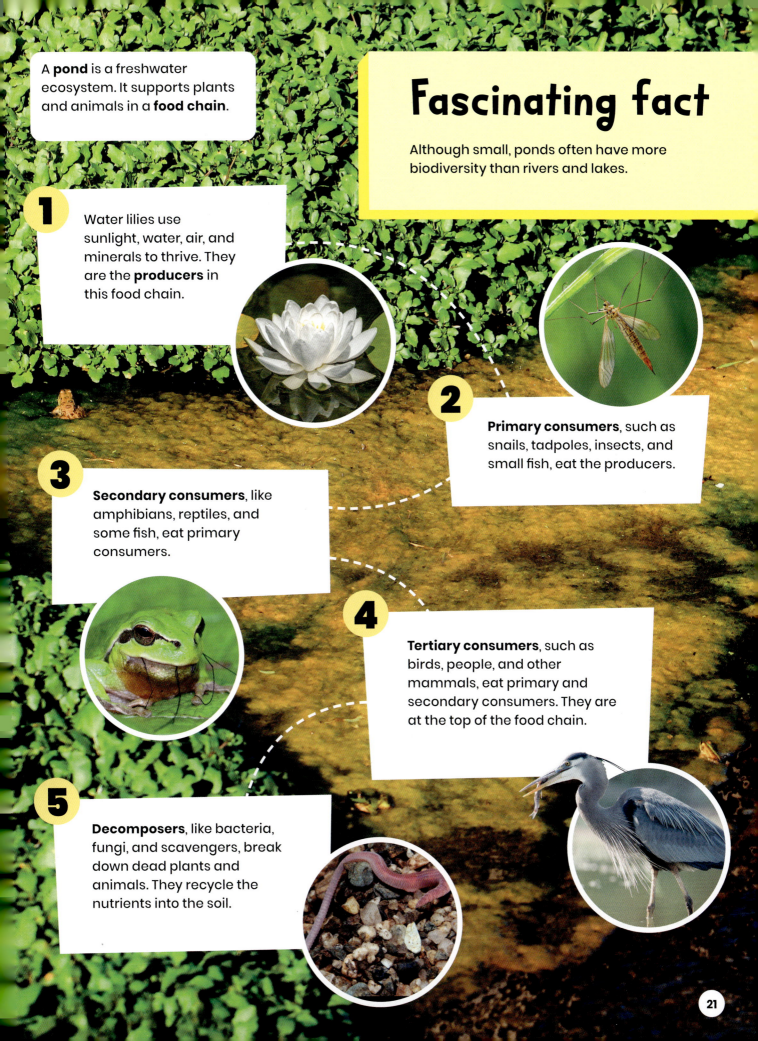

Case Study: THE GANGES

One of the world's great rivers, the Ganges starts in the Himalayas. It flows through India and Bangladesh for about 1,557 miles (2,506 km). The Ganges has many **tributaries**. These join with other rivers to form a huge basin of fertile land. Hundreds of millions people depend on the Ganges for food and water.

The Ganges is also known as "the disappearing river." In some places, it flows underground before reappearing!

Ganges river dolphins are blind. They hunt for food by making high-pitched sounds. The sounds bounce off prey, which helps the dolphins locate them.

Fascinating fact

Nearly 2,500 years ago, a huge earthquake moved the course of the Ganges River 28 miles (45 km) away.

The river is an important spiritual site.

The Ganges floods each year during **monsoon** season. The floodwater moves rich soil from the river to the land. Crops like rice, wheat, sugarcane, and cotton grow in the fertile land.

Rhesus monkeys make the most of living in an ecosystem alongside humans. They hunt through garbage for leftover food.

People and industry have heavily polluted the Ganges. There are major efforts to remove trash from the surface and stop the flow of sewage into the river.

Marine ECOSYSTEMS

Almost all the water on Earth (97 percent) is found in the oceans. Earth's oceans are home to many vibrant marine ecosystems. These saltwater habitats can be found in the open ocean, along the coast, and even on the ocean floor.

An estuary is a marine ecosystem. It forms where a river meets the ocean. The Chesapeake Bay is one example. Many animals live there, including osprey, great blue herons, sturgeon, and blue crabs.

Coral reefs are some of the most colorful marine ecosystems on Earth.

Scientists have discovered hot vents on the floor of every ocean. They are formed when seawater is super-heated by magma in Earth's crust. The hot water shoots out of gaps in the ocean floor.

As the hot water meets cold water, minerals in the water turn solid. Hot vents are some of the most unusual habitats on Earth.

Hundreds of species of animals, like vent mussels, live near hot vents.

Kelp is a large algae that grows in cold, nutrient-rich seawater. Thousands of fish, invertebrates, and marine mammals use kelp for shelter and food.

Fascinating fact

The largest kelp forest grows along the southern coasts of Chile and Argentina. It is around 620 miles (1,000 km) long.

25

Case Study: THE GREAT BARRIER REEF

The Great Barrier Reef is located on the northeast coast of Australia. It is the largest coral reef in the world. It can even be seen from space! The reef is home to over 600 species of coral and over 1,500 species of fish. But the reef faces threats, like pollution and **coral bleaching**.

The box jellyfish is one of more than 100 species of jellyfish living in the reef. Its venom is the deadliest in the world.

Over 130 species of sharks live in the reef, including tiny epaulette sharks and fearsome tiger sharks.

As seawater temperatures rise due to climate change, corals expel the algae that live inside them. This causes them to turn white. Bleached corals are at risk of dying.

Plastics, runoff from farming, and fuel spills from ships pollute the reef. This harms the growth and reproduction of corals.

Fascinating fact

Black corals live in deep sea reefs. They can live for more than 4,000 years.

Scientists are working to restore damaged reefs. They remove small pieces of coral and plant them back in the reef. They also breed new corals and use them to **repopulate** the reef.

Desert ECOSYSTEMS

The Mojave Desert in California is cool in the winter and hot in the summer.

A dry or **arid** environment is known as a desert ecosystem. This is caused by low **precipitation**. Deserts get less than 10 inches (25 cm) of rain a year. They experience extreme temperatures. Many people think of deserts as hot places. But there are also cold deserts.

Namib sand geckos hunt at night and have large eyes to help them see their prey. By morning, dew collects on their eyes, which they lick off to stay **hydrated**.

Bactrian camels live in the Gobi Desert. They can cope with temperatures between 104°F (40°C) and -22°F (-30°C). The camels get energy from the fat in their two humps.

Fascinating fact

Antarctica is the windiest desert on Earth. The wind can toss a snowmobile weighing 800 pounds (362 kg) across the ice.

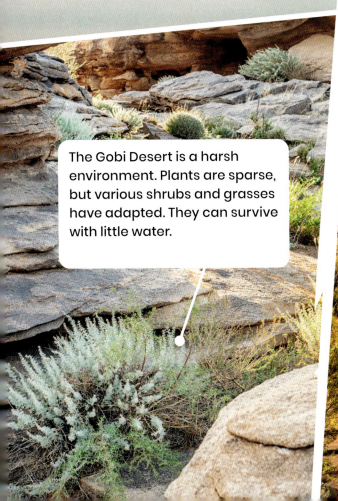

Andean flamingos thrive in the cold Atacama Desert, which is the driest desert in the world. They survive on food and water in the salt flat pools.

Antarctica is a cold desert. The average temperature is −70°F (−57°C). While the seas that surround Antarctica are full of life, the desert has little biodiversity.

The Gobi Desert is a harsh environment. Plants are sparse, but various shrubs and grasses have adapted. They can survive with little water.

The saguaro cactus is only found in the Sonoran Desert in North America. It stores water in its stem and arms. Its hard spines protect it from animals.

Case Study: THE SAHARA

The Sahara Desert is the largest hot desert in the world. It spans 3,000 miles (4,800 km) across North Africa and touches 11 countries. It is one of the most arid places on Earth. Sometimes, it does not rain there for years. It is also very hot. In the summer, temperatures regularly top 104°F (40°C).

Sahara sand viper snakes spend their days burrowed beneath the surface of the ground to stay cool and watch for prey. They have sharp-edged scales that help them wriggle into the sand with amazing speed.

The Sahara Desert is mostly rock. But 30 percent of the landscape is sand. The impressive sand dunes can reach heights of 500 ft (152 m).

Fascinating fact

Archaeologists have found rock art in the Sahara that dates back over 9,000 years. Based on the animals in the art, scientists think the area was much greener and wetter than it is now.

Date palms are found near fertile **oasis** ecosystems. They need heat to bear fruit, but can survive short periods below freezing.

The Laperrine's olive tree grows high in the mountains of the Sahara Desert. It can survive in extremely dry conditions.

The addax, or white antelope, is well adapted to the Sahara Desert. It eats shrubs and can go months without water.

The fennec fox is the smallest fox in the world. Its huge ears help it stay cool and find prey.

Helping ECOSYSTEMS

Not everyone can help restore the Great Barrier Reef or stop deforestation in the Amazon. But we can all conserve nature where we live. Every positive action can help the plants and animals in a habitat. Take a look outside. What can you do in your ecosystem?

Collecting rainwater is a great way to conserve water. You can use it to water indoor and outdoor plants. And it is free!

Planting trees helps fight climate change, as trees capture and store carbon dioxide. This slows the buildup of carbon dioxide in the atmosphere. Trees are also important habitats for many animals.

32

We need pollinators like bees for much of our food to grow. But habitat loss and pesticide use decrease their numbers. Pollinator gardens provide spaces for these insects to eat, shelter, and breed.

Litter is one cause of air, water, and land pollution. Trash releases toxins that harm living organisms. By regularly picking up litter, we can keep our ecosystem healthier.

Making a compost pile limits how much waste goes to a landfill. It creates fertile soil for plants as it recycles nutrients.

We can grow our own food in vegetable gardens or allotments. Vegetable gardens are great habitats for ladybugs, worms, toads, snakes, bees, and microorganisms.

33

Everyday SCIENCE

Taking the Wolves out of Yellowstone

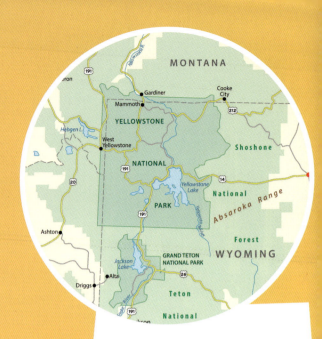

In Yellowstone National Park, living creatures interact with the landscape without much human interference. But this has not always been so. In the 1900s, people started a campaign to get rid of the wolves of Yellowstone. This had a huge effect on the ecosystem.

Yellowstone became a national park in 1872. It covers parts of Wyoming, Montana, and Idaho.

Ranchers feared that the Yellowstone wolves would escape and destroy their livestock. To stop this, people were encouraged to kill the wolves.

The last wolf pack was killed in 1926. This threw the ecosystem out of balance.

Without gray wolves, the number of elk went up. Wolves were one of their main predators. Elk are herbivores. They eat shrubs, small trees, lichens, flowers, and ferns.

As the number of elk increased, the vegetation they ate decreased. Willow, cotton, and ash trees started to disappear from the park.

Everyday SCIENCE
Rewilding Yellowstone

Rewilding is a form of conservation. It restores an area of land to its wild state. It often involves reintroducing a species that became extinct. When the wolves were removed from Yellowstone, it caused a dramatic change to the food chain. Ecologists realized that they needed to reintroduce wolves to the ecosystem.

In 1995, eight gray wolves from Canada were reintroduced to Yellowstone. By the end of 1996, 31 wolves were in the park and surrounding area.

Ecologists built three pens to house 14 wolves to help them get used to their new surroundings. After a few weeks, they released the wolves into the wild.

BEFORE

AFTER

Having wolves back in Yellowstone helped to rebalance the ecosystem. After their return, there were fewer elk and more trees.

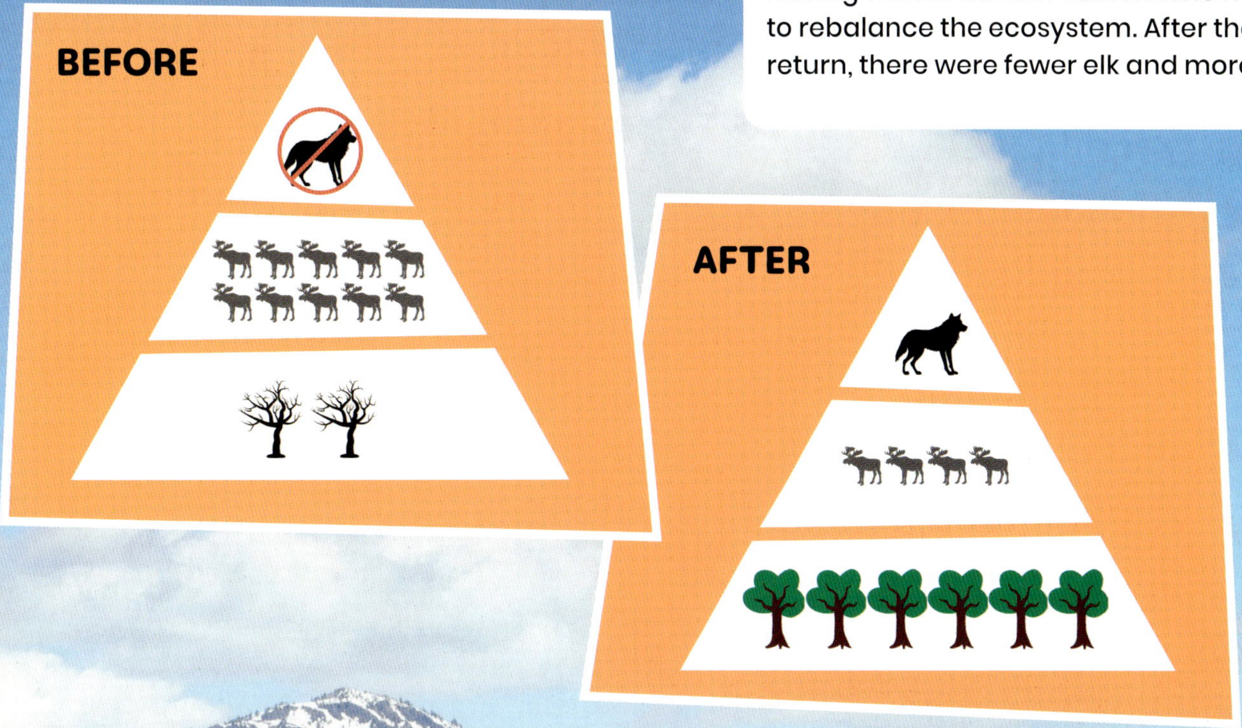

Today, Yellowstone is a thriving biodiverse ecosystem. But it faces a new danger—climate change. With rising temperatures, the risk of fire increases. This threat impacts the wetlands, grasslands, and animals that live in the national park.

REWILDING BEAVERS

Beavers were hunted to extinction in the UK. They have since been successfully introduced in England and Scotland through rewilding.

37

Let's EXPERIMENT!

BUILDING FOR BEES

Bees are vital to many of Earth's ecosystems. They like to build nests and lay eggs somewhere safe and sheltered. You can help the bees in your area by building them their own hotel.

You will need:
- Scissors
- A large plastic bottle
- Bamboo stems
- String

Ask an adult to cut the plastic bottle and bamboo stems.

1 Cut the top and bottom off a large plastic bottle.

2 Cut the bamboo stems so they are the same length as the middle section of the bottle.

3 Fill the middle section of the bottle with the bamboo stems.

4 Tightly tie two pieces of string around the bottle so the stems are secure. Hang your bee hotel outside. See who comes to stay!

A BEE COLLECTING NECTAR

Bees fly from flower to flower to eat nectar. As they do, they leave pollen from one flower in the next flower. The pollen helps the flowers make new seeds.

39

Let's EXPERIMENT!

MAKE A BIRD FEEDER

Birds live in lots of ecosystems around the world. You can encourage them to visit your outdoor space by making an owl-shaped bird feeder for them to eat from.

You will need:
- A cardboard carton
- Scissors
- Paint and glue to decorate
- Birdseed
- A straw
- String

Ask an adult to cut the carton.

40

1 Cut a semi-circle out of the front of the carton and a small hole under the semi-circle. Then, cut two more semi-circles on each side of the carton.

2 Leave the cardboard attached at the top to form two flaps so they look like wings.

3 Use the paint to decorate your carton so it looks like a bird! Use the cardboard cut off from the carton to make a beak. Glue this on your carton.

4 Put some birdseed in the bottom of the carton. Insert a straw in the small hole for birds to land on. Attach the string and hang your finished bird feeder outside!

A STARLING LOOKING FOR FOOD

Birds are found in diverse habitats all around the world. They are important parts of forest, grassland, desert, and urban ecosystems.

Vocabulary BUILDER

What Does an Ecologist Do?

An ecologist is a scientist. They study how living things interact with their environments and how these change over time. They take samples, watch wildlife, and collect data. Sometimes they are outside and other times they work in labs and offices.

MY LIFE AS AN ECOLOGIST

I love being an ecologist! I study how different species affect ecosystems to help protect our environment.

I work with colleagues, including other scientists. We share ideas on how to protect environments and think of ways that we can tackle climate change together.

My favorite thing is to observe an ecosystem, taking notes on what I see and testing samples. I use sustainable methods, such as planting trees and cleaning rivers, to help make a difference.

I also collaborate with workers from governments, industries, and charities to create rules to help with conservation.

42

What an ecologist does: advise, assess, collaborate, conserve, design, investigate, manage, observe, predict, preserve, protect, restore, study, test

Interests of an ecologist: animals, climate change, ecosystems, environments, food chains, food webs, habitats, government policies, human development, invasive species, land, plants, predator–prey relationships, water

Imagine you are an ecologist. Use the words in the vocabulary box above and the example on page 42 to describe what you do in a typical day of work.

Think about:

- Which ecosystems you study
- Where you work
- Who you talk to and why

Glossary

Abiotic Non-living.

Adaptation The process in which a plant or animal changes as a result of its environment to help it survive or reproduce.

Arctic One of the world's climate zones, found at the poles.

Arid Very dry, with little to no rainfall.

Biodiversity The variety of living things in a habitat or ecosystem.

Biotic Living.

Camouflage Colored or shaped in such a way to blend in with the surroundings.

Canopy The top layer of foliage formed by the trees in a forest.

Carnivore An animal that only eats meat.

Cloud forest A tropical forest that has cooler temperatures, a mountainous location, and lots of clouds, that produce precipitation.

Condense To change from a gas or vapor to a liquid.

Conservation The act of preserving and protecting a habitat or ecosystem.

Continent One of the seven great landmasses on Earth.

Coral bleaching The process in which corals expel the algae that live inside them and turn white, due to the rising temperature of seawater as a result of climate change.

Coral reef An underwater structure made up of tiny sea creatures called corals.

Decomposer A living thing that breaks down dead matter, recycling its nutrients in the soil.

Deforestation The act of cutting down trees in a forest, which reduces the overall amount of forest.

Diverse Including many different types of things.

Ecologist A scientist who studies the relationships between living things and their environment.

Ecosystem A community of living things that interact with non-living things in their environment.

Endangered Used to describe an animal or plant that is in danger of going extinct.

Equator An imaginary line around Earth, halfway between the North Pole and the South Pole.

Evaporate To turn from a liquid into steam, vapor or gas.

Food chain A group of living things that eat one another in an ecosystem, allowing energy to flow between them.

Forest A large area covered in trees.

Grassland A wide and open expanse of grasses, shrubs, and few trees, found in the temperate and tropical zones.

Habitat An environment where plants, animals, and other organisms live.

Herbivore An animal that only eats plants.

Humidity The amount of water vapor in the air.

Hydrated Having enough water to stay healthy.

Iridescent Used to describe something that is glowing, shiny, and brightly colored.

Lake A body of fresh water or salt water surrounded by land.

Monsoon A shift in winds that brings huge amounts of precipitation to tropical areas.

Northern lights Lights in the night sky, near the North Pole, created when particles from the Sun mix with gases in Earth's atmosphere.

Oasis A fertile area made by a source of fresh water in a dry region.

Oceanographer A scientist who studies the ocean.

Photosynthesis A process in which green plants, algae, and some bacteria use sunlight to make oxygen and energy.

Pond A small body of fresh water with no moving water.

Precipitation When water vapor or moisture falls from the clouds as rain, sleet, snow, or hail.

Predator An animal that hunts and eats another animal.

Prey An animal that is hunted and eaten by another animal.

Primary consumer A living thing that eats producers.

Producer A living thing, such as a plant or algae, that uses energy from the Sun to get its nutrients.

Rainforest A forest found in the tropical or temperate zones that is characterized by high humidity and high rainfall.

Repopulate To increase numbers of a species after they have previously declined.

Rewilding To return land and oceans to their natural or wilder states.

River A large stream of fresh water that flows into a body of water.

Savanna A type of grassland found in the tropical zone.

Season A period of the year characterized by certain weather and temperature conditions.

Secondary consumer A living thing that eats primary consumers.

Species A group of living things that have similar features and can produce offspring.

Stream A natural flow of water that is smaller than a river.

Temperate One of the world's climate zones, found between the tropical and Arctic zones.

Tertiary consumer A living thing that eats primary and secondary consumers.

Tributary A small stream that flows into a main river.

Tropical One of the world's climate zones, found near the equator.

Wetland An area of land where water covers the soil, either year-round or part of the year.

Woodland An area covered in trees, but less densely than in a forest.

Index

A
addax (white antelope) 31

Amazon 10–11, 32

Andean flamingos 29

Antarctica 29

arapaima fish 11

Atacama Desert 29

B
beavers 12, 39

bees 33, 38–39

Big Five 19

bird feeder experiment 40–41

birds
    quetzal 8

    starlings 41

bison 18

boreal forest 14

box jellyfish 26

brown bears 15

brushtail possum 17

C
cacao trees 11

Canadian lynx 14

capybaras 10

carnivores 19

Carson, Rachel 6

caves 4

climate change 27, 32, 37

cloud forests 8–9

clouded leopards 9

coast redwoods trees 12

compost piles 33

consumers, primary/ secondary/tertiary 21

coral reefs 24, 26–27

D
date palms 31

decomposers 21

deforestation 10

desert ecosystems 28–29

dromedary camels 28

E
ecologists 6, 42–43

ecosystems
    defined 4–5

    helping 32–33

ecotourism 18

elk 35

estuaries 24

eucalyptus trees 17

experiments
  bee hotels 38–39

  bird feeders 40–41

F
fennec foxes 31

fireweed 15

flood plains 7

forests 6
    cloud 8–9

    temperate 12–13

    temperate rainforests 12–13

    tropical rainforests 7, 8–9

foxes 4, 31

freshwater ecosystems 20–21

G
Ganges 22–23

gardening 33

giant water lilies 11

Gobi desert 29

grasslands 16–17

Great Barrier Reef 26–27, 32

H
habitats 4, 32, 33

herbivores 19

hot vents 25

J
jellyfish 26

K

kelp 25

L

Laperrine's olive tree 31

leaf-cutter ants 11

leopards 9

limnologists 20

litter 33

M

maple trees 9

marine ecosystems 7, 24–25

Mojave Desert 28

monsoons 22

muskeg 15

N

Namid sand geckos 28

Northern Lights 14

O

oasis ecosystems 31

orangutans 9

oxpeckers 19

P

pollution 23, 26, 27, 33

ponds 21

prairie dogs 18

producers 21

pufferfish 5

purple pitcher plants 15

Q

quetzal 8

R

rainforests

    temperate 12–13

    tropical 7, 8–9, 13

recreation 7

rewilding, Yellowstone National Park 36–37

rhesus monkeys 23

rhinoceroses 19

river dolphins 22

rock art 30

S

saguaro cactus 29

Sahara Desert 30–31

savannas 16–17

Serengeti 18–19

sharks 26

snowshoe hares 12

Sonoran Desert 29

spikethumb frogs 8

starlings 41

T

taiga 14–15

temperate forests/rainforests 12–13

tigers 9

toucans 5

trees 32

    cacao 11

    coast redwoods 12

    date palms 31

    eucalyptus 17

    helping ecosystems 32

    Laperrine's olive 31

    maple 9

tropical rainforests 7, 8–9, 13

tundras 6

V

vent mussels 25

viper snakes 30

W

whiptail wallabies 17

wildebeest 19

wolves 34–7

Y

Yellowstone National Park 34–37

Acknowledgments

The publisher would like to thank the following for their kind permission to reproduce their photographs:

(Key: a-above; b-below/bottom; c-center; f-far; l-left; r-right; t-top)

123RF.com: 1xpert 6-7c, Dennis van de Water 13b, Richard Whitcombe 27tr; **Alamy Stock Photo:** Arterra Picture Library / Arndt Sven-Erik 15r, William Berry 21ca, Frank Bienewald 23tl, 23bl, BIOSPHOTO / Tobias Bernhard Raff 25b, blickwinkel / H. Duty 21clb, Ger Bosma 10cb, Mike Cavaroc 35b, Sue Cunningham 10cr, Danita Delimont / Ellen B. Goff 29bl, Reinhard Dirscherl 5br, Redmond Durrell 11cla, John Dvorak 28, Alison Eckett 23br, Jonathan Eden 35cl, FLPA 8clb, Norma Jean Gargasz 33br, geoffwiggins.com 31tl, GH Photos 33tl, Thijs de Graaf 32cb, Diego Grandi 29tl, Greenshoots Communications / GS International 42crb, Frank Hecker 15clb, Nigel Housden 21cra, Scott Hurd 28cr, imageBROKER.com GmbH & Co. KG / Fabian von Poser 18cra, Heather King 36b, Matthijs Kuijpers 30crb, William Leaman 41br, Frans Lemmens 4tr, Rainer Lesniewski 34tr, Suzanne Long 27b, Miceking 37 (Tree), Cyril Ruoso / Minden Pictures 9bl, Michael Durham / Minden Pictures 12cra, Alejandro Miranda 5tr, William Mullins 20cb, Nature Picture Library / Wild Wonders of Europe / Lundgren 21bc, Boyd Norton 16cb, NPS Photo / Jacob W. Frank via Planetpix 34b, Ihor Obraztsov 37 (Elk), Panther Media GmbH / Nico Smit 31bl, Park Collection 36clb, Sean Pavone 32-33c, Trevor Penfold 7bl, Wiliam Perry 12crb, PG Arphexad 32bl, Rolf Nussbaumer Photography 21br, Feodora Rosca 37 (Wolf), Heather Rose 19tl, Science History Images 43c, Science History Images / Photo Researchers 25tl, 25tr, Anil Shakya 23tr, Taina Sohlman 6br, Miguel Lasa / Steve Bloom Images 26clb, Alexey Stiop 20b, Daniel Thornberg 37, Tierfotoagentur / M. Zindl 9br, Ann and Steve Toon 19br, Alan Dyer / VWPics 14, Roy Waller 37bl, WaterFrame_dpr 24, Thomas Weber 35t, Jim West 33cb, Zoonar / Aleksandr Kurganov 11bl; **Dorling Kindersley:** Mark Winwood / RHS Wisley 17l; **Dreamstime. com:** Mihai Andritoiu 24cra, Antonel 29br, Valentin Armianu / Asterixvs 30, Achim Baqué 6c, Bounder32h 15tl, Siarhei Dzmitryienka 7cra, Empire331 5tl, Andrey Gudkov 19tr, Tatsiana Hendzel 9t, Tracy Immordino 15bl, Debra James 7clb, Emanuele Mazzoni 31tr, Outdoorsman 14crb, Sean Pavone 12, Dmitry Pichugin 28clb, Pilshik 15cla, Pniesen 26cra, Saaaaa 4b, Stephan Scherhag 8, Nalidsa Sukprasert 13t, Tolly81 26, Tomonishi 9cr, Travellingtobeprecise 4bc, Tzooka 31br, David Pereiras Villagra 33cra, Imogen Warren 17br, Marc Witte 17tr, Zenistock 22b, Andrii Zhezhera 21; **Getty Images:** Londolozi Images / Mint Images 19bl, Juan Carlos Vindas 8crb; **Getty Images / iStock:** goinyk 29tr, KenCanning 16, lightpix 16cra, PhotoTalk 7tl, pierivb 18b; **Shutterstock.com:** Ethan Daniels 27tl, Binoy B Gogoi 22c, mapman 10b, 11r

Cover images: *Front:* **Dreamstime.com:** Silvael cr; **Getty Images:** Moment / © Jackie Bale bl; **Shutterstock.com:** Malchevska br, SaveJungle t; *Back:* **Alamy Stock Photo:** Redmond Durrell bl, Diego Grandi tl; **Dreamstime.com:** Tomonishi cl